Your

Travel

Guide to

CIVIL WAR
AMERICA

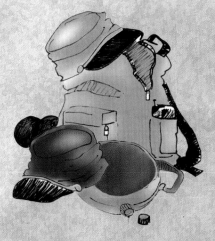

Your Travel Guide to CIVIL WAR AMERICA

Nancy Day

RUNESTONE PRESS • MINNEAPOLIS

AN IMPRINT OF LERNER PUBLISHING GROUP

Designed by: Zachary Marell and Tim Parlin
Edited by: Sara Saetre and Martha Kranes
Illustrated by: Tim Parlin
Photo Researched by: Cynthia Zemlicka

Runestone Press
An imprint of Lerner Publishing Group
241 First Avenue North
Minneapolis, Minnesota 55401 U.S.A.

Website address: www.lernerbooks.com

Library of Congress Cataloging-in-Publication Data

Day, Nancy.
    Your travel guide to Civil War America / by Nancy Day.
    p.   cm. — (Passport to history)
    Includes bibliographical references and index.
    Summary: Takes readers on a journey back in time in order to experience life
during the Civil War, describing clothing, accommodations, food, local customs,
transportation, a few notable personalities, and more.
    ISBN 0-8225-3078-3 (lib. bdg. : alk. paper)
    1. United States—History—Civil War, 1861–1865 Juvenile literature. 2. United
States—Social life and customs—1783–1865 Juvenile literature. 3. United States
Guidebooks Juvenile literature. [1. United States—History—Civil War, 1861–1865.
2. United States—Social life and customs—1783–1865.] I. Title. II. Series: Day,
Nancy. Passport to history.
E468.9.D29   2001   99-37097
973.7—dc21

Manufactured in the United States of America
1 2 3 4 5 6 – JR – 06 05 04 03 02 01

CONTENTS

INTRODUCTION

GETTING STARTED

Welcome to Passport to History. You will be traveling through time and space to Civil War America. A civil war is a war between two opposing groups within one nation. In Civil War America, you'll find the United States of America bitterly divided between the North and the South. The war lasted from April 12, 1861, to April 9, 1865. This guide will answer questions such as:

- ➤ **Where should I stay?**
- ➤ **What should I see?**
- ➤ **Who should I meet during my visit?**
- ➤ **How do I stay safe but also see the war up close?**

Remember, you are going back in time. Some of the things to which you are accustomed—such as TV—didn't yet exist. So forget packing your video games, hair dryer, medicines, and other modern conveniences that would make your stay a lot more comfortable. Modern cameras won't work here either. Photography was in its early stages during the Civil War. But cameras were very different from the

A blockade runs through the yard of this Atlanta, Georgia, home. The Civil War is literally fought in people's backyards.

ones you're used to. They were big and clumsy. They didn't have features such as automatic focusing that made them easy to use. Ordinary people left photography to the professionals. But don't worry. The locals do just fine without all of these gadgets, and with a little help from this book, you will too.

THE UNION (NORTH) AND THE CONFEDERACY (SOUTH), 1861

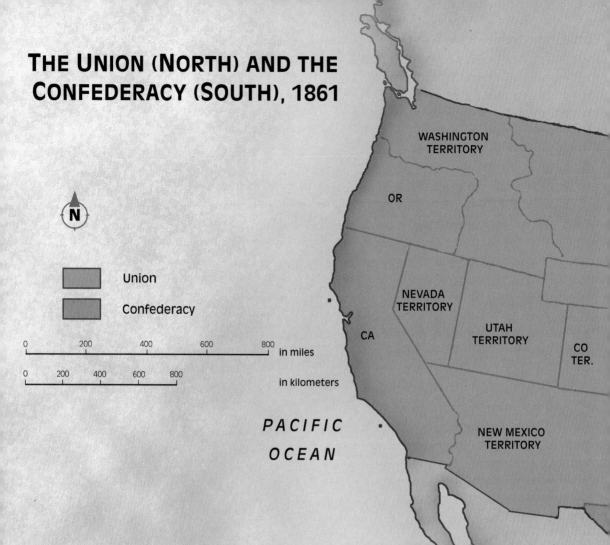

N

Union

Confederacy

| 0 | 200 | 400 | 600 | 800 |
in miles

| 0 | 200 | 400 | 600 | 800 |
in kilometers

WASHINGTON
TERRITORY

OR

NEVADA
TERRITORY

UTAH
TERRITORY

CO
TER.

CA

NEW MEXICO
TERRITORY

PACIFIC
OCEAN

NOTE TO THE TRAVELER

Use this guide as a resource for what to expect during
your visit to Civil War America. Some of the information comes from people who lived during this time. They
wrote letters, diaries, newspaper articles, and many other
firsthand reports.

Much information comes from historians, archaeologists, and other
modern experts. They have studied documents, photographs, artworks,
buildings, tools, and various things from this era. These modern sleuths
use these clues to interpret the way things might have been.

Traveling back in time will give you an advantage historians and archaeologists don't have. You can compare what's in our history books to
the way things really were.

BRITISH NORTH AMERICA

DAKOTA
TERRITORY

MN

WI

MI

ME

VT

NH

NY

MA

CT

RI

PA

Washington, D.C.

NJ

DE

IA

Chicago

NEBRASKA
TERRITORY

OH

IL

IN

CO
TER.

KS

MO

KY

VA

Richmond

MD

TN

NC

INDIAN
TERRITORY

AR

SC

TX

MS

AL

GA

ATLANTIC
OCEAN

LA

FL

WHY VISIT CIVIL WAR AMERICA?

The Civil War was anything but civil (polite). An estimated 690,000 people died during the war. Some died in battle or in accidents, but about 425,000 died from disease. In the crowded army camps and hospitals, disease spread easily.

The Civil War began after eleven states—South Carolina, Georgia, Alabama, Mississippi, Florida, Louisiana, Texas, North Carolina, Tennessee, Arkansas, and Virginia—seceded (withdrew) from the United

In South Carolina, slaves return from the cotton fields bearing loads of freshly picked cotton. On January 1, 1863, Lincoln declares slavery illegal in South Carolina. Jefferson Davis, president of the Confederacy, disagrees, however. He considers slavery legal.

States. These Southern states formed their own nation, the Confederate States of America. The Confederacy elected Jefferson Davis as president.

In some Northern states, slavery was illegal. Many Yankees (Northerners) wanted to make slavery illegal in every state. But only a few Southerners opposed slavery. The Southern economy relied on slaves. Slaves did most of the work on huge Southern farms called plantations. Plantation owners spent a lot of money to buy slaves.

The states in the North were known as the Union. They were led by President Abraham Lincoln. Lincoln believed states did not have the right to secede. He was willing to fight to keep the nation together. Not all Northerners supported Lincoln and the war. But most did.

When the war began, neither the North nor the South was ready. The Union had only a small regular army. As a brand new nation, the Confederacy had no army. Both sides needed to enlist tens of thousands of men as soon as possible. In addition, Northern factories had to stop making peacetime goods and start making weapons. Cloth was sewn into uniforms instead of everyday clothes. Farmers sent their crops to feed soldiers.

Soldiers fought in cities and on farms, in backyards and in public places. Because the war wasn't confined to a battlefield, many civilians were killed or wounded. Most of the fighting took place in the South, so visiting the Southern states will be especially dangerous.

The longer the war went on, the more it took a toll. So the later you travel, the harder the journey. Although this trip is hardly a tourist's dream vacation, it is worth the effort. The Civil War was a critical turning point in American history. It kept the United States together as one nation. It helped end slavery. It influenced what kind of nation the United States of America eventually became. Your trip to Civil War America will make you an eyewitness to this remarkable time.

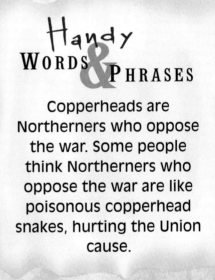

Handy WORDS & PHRASES

Copperheads are Northerners who oppose the war. Some people think Northerners who oppose the war are like poisonous copperhead snakes, hurting the Union cause.

THE BASICS

Bodies of soldiers lie in a field after the Battle of Antietam, which takes place in 1862 near Maryland's border with Virginia.

LOCATION LOWDOWN

Some battles of the Civil War take place in the North. But many are fought in the South, especially after the North begins to win the war and march into Southern territory. States in the Midwest and the West send men to fight in the war. But civilians in those areas are safe.

In the North, you'll find many small farms. But you'll also find big cities bustling with activity. Huge factories and mills are pumping out goods such as cloth, furniture, and farm equipment. Newly built ships and trains take these goods all around the nation and the world.

Streams of immigrants are pouring in from Europe. Thousands settle in Eastern port cities such as New York. In the West, over 150,000 Chinese immigrants have arrived. Many are working on the railroads or in the mines. Immigrants are willing to work long hours for low pay. For this reason, the North has little need of slave labor.

The South is largely rural. It has few towns of any size and no really large cities. Mostly you'll find rolling hills, woods, and vast plantation fields. The main crops are tobacco and cotton. Slaves do most of the work of planting, harvesting, and baling. Slaves also work in the huge plantation homes, which need many hands to run smoothly.

Most able-bodied men have enlisted (joined the military). Others have been drafted (ordered to serve). Away from the battlefields (particularly in the South), you'll mostly meet women, children, elderly or disabled men, and slaves. Almost every family has a father, brother, husband, or son in the war.

You'll find more hardship in the South than in the North. The South relies on Northern factories for many goods. Since Southerners mostly grow tobacco and cotton, they also depend on the North for food. During the war, the North stops selling food and goods to the South. President Lincoln also orders a blockade of all Southern ports. The blockade begins on April 19, 1861, and continues until the end of the war. It prevents foreign countries from shipping supplies to the Confederacy and the Confederacy from selling its goods abroad.

TAKE IT from a Local

There is a vacant chair in every house.
—*Lizzie Hardin, a Kentucky girl writing in her diary*

Soldiers from both armies forage (steal supplies) as they travel along. They fill wagons with hams, flour, corn, sweet potatoes, chickens, and other food. They help themselves to cattle, mules, horses, saddles, and wagons. Army commanders don't usually allow foraging. But it is still a major source of supplies for both armies.

Blockade runners (boats that try to slip through the blockade) do get some goods in and out of the South. Even so, many common things—such as ink, candles, kerosene, and buttons—become scarce. Locals make do with what they have. In a pinch, berry juice works as ink. A twisted rag can serve as a candle. Cottonseed oil and ground peas replace kerosene for fueling lamps.

You'll find far more destruction in the South than in the North. Soldiers and horses trudge through fields, trampling crops and tearing down fences. They march through towns, stealing and damaging people's belongings. The locals suffer even more when a battle takes place on their property.

SLAVERY

In 1860 about half a million African Americans are free. Some were born free. Others bought their freedom or were freed by their owners. But about four million African Americans are slaves. One in every seven Americans is owned by someone.

Most slaves live in the South. Field slaves till soil, plant crops, pick cotton, and harvest rice and tobacco. They work until dark unless there is a full moon, in which case they must continue working. House slaves tend children, cook and serve food, haul wood, and perform other tasks. Slave children also work. They may be sent to the fields at age twelve.

Household slaves sweep a courtyard of a white homestead.

During the war, the Confederate army uses slaves to do noncombat jobs. Confederate soldiers are then free for war service. Slaves build fortifications, work on railroads, and do other heavy work. Some Confederate soldiers take slaves with them as servants.

Most slaves live in one-room shacks or barrack-style buildings on the grounds of a plantation. These buildings have dirt floors, sparse furnishings, and flimsy walls that let in drafts. Diseases such as pneumonia,

Back TO THE FUTURE

Many Northerners believe slavery is wrong. But most are not abolitionists (people who want to end slavery). Very few people believe that African Americans are equal to whites. The struggle for equal rights for African Americans continues in modern times.

typhus, cholera, and tuberculosis spread easily in the cramped and dirty conditions.

Slaves are prisoners to the whims of their masters. They are sold like livestock. Families may be split up, with the husband, wife, and children being sold to different owners. A slave who won't obey or do a job to a master's satisfaction may be whipped, tortured, or even killed. Occasionally slaves are allowed to buy their freedom, or they are freed by their owners. Most remain in bondage until the end of the Civil War.

Handy Words & Phrases

A newly freed slave is referred to as contraband.

CLIMATE

Climate plays an important role in the Civil War. You'll notice the same differences in climate that exist in modern times. The North has a colder climate and a shorter growing season. Farms are smaller. Farmers grow crops that can be planted and harvested by one family. With fewer

Two women wash and iron in front of their slave quarters.

16

people on farms, Northerners turn to big cities and factories to make a living.

The South has a warmer climate. The growing season is longer. Tobacco, cotton, rice, and other warm climate crops thrive here. The South's agricultural economy is based on these crops. The growth of huge plantations leads to the need for large numbers of cheap workers. Wealthy Southerners come to rely heavily on slaves. So in a sense, climate differences help to pave the way for the Civil War.

ENLISTING IN THE ARMY

If you are especially adventurous, you may wish to try life as a soldier. Both armies say you have to be male to enlist. But about four hundred women try to enlist, disguising themselves as men. Some succeed in becoming soldiers. (One Union general was astonished when one of his sergeants had a baby!) Women who try to enlist want to be near their soldier husbands. Or they want to fight because they believe in the cause.

Many boys under age eighteen become soldiers. Both armies have rules forbidding boys younger than eighteen from enlisting. Even so, about 10 to 20 percent of soldiers in both armies are underage. About ten thousand Union soldiers are probably younger than eighteen. Nearly five hundred are probably

Union soldier Frances Clalin is one of dozens of female soldiers fighting in the Civil War.

younger than fifteen. One boy, Charles Carter Hay, joins the Confederate army in 1861 at age eleven. You might be able to slip into the army, too. The armies can't easily check your age (social security cards, driver's licenses, and computerized records don't exist).

At the beginning of the war, Confederate soldiers enlist for a term of twelve months. By 1862, however, the army's numbers have dwindled. The Confederacy gives its president the power to draft any man between eighteen and thirty-five. These soldiers must serve until the war ends. There are a few exceptions, however. An owner or overseer of twenty or more slaves cannot be called for military service. Also, free African Americans can only serve as musicians. The Confederacy does not accept free blacks as soldiers.

In the Union, President Lincoln asks men to volunteer for three years. Not enough men do this, however. So the Union starts to draft men in 1863. Each state raises its own regiments. If a state signs up enough volunteers for three-year terms, that state doesn't have to draft anyone. For this reason, states offer cash bounties to volunteers. Most Union soldiers join to collect the cash.

In both the North and the South, well-to-do men have an advantage. They don't have to fight, even if they are drafted. They are allowed to hire substitutes to take their place. Poorer people in some places resent this.

At first the Union doesn't let African Americans become soldiers. Most Northern whites are fighting to preserve the Union, not to free slaves. Despite this attitude, many African Americans are eager to help in the war effort. On October 28, 1862, the first African American regiment—the 79th U.S. Colored Infantry—goes into battle.

If you want to enlist, report to a recruiting office (look for signs calling for volunteers). Don't sweat the physical examination—it's often a joke. Fast, careless physical exams are what make it possible for some women to sneak into the army disguised as men.

Next you'll be asked to pledge allegiance to your side, the Confederacy or the United States. Ask someone to help you learn the pledge. Neither pledge is the same as the one you know from modern times (which was written in the 1890s). You'll also promise to obey orders and abide by the articles of war for your side.

Twenty-seven soldiers of Company E, 4th U.S. Colored Infantry, pose with rifles at Fort Lincoln in Washington, D.C.

19

WHICH CITIES TO VISIT

WASHINGTON, D.C.

Washington, D.C., is the capital of the United States. It is also the seat (capital) of the Union. When you arrive, you'll immediately notice the Capitol building. Its shiny new dome was being constructed when Abraham Lincoln took his oath of office in March 1861. He rode to his inauguration in a horse and buggy.

The beautiful Potomac River snakes its way along Washington's border. Across the Potomac is Virginia, a Confederate state. Soldiers from both armies (about 250,000 in 1862) are camped along both sides of the river. Forts dot the river bluffs. The home of Robert E. Lee (who becomes the general in chief of all Confederate armies) overlooks Washington from the Virginia side of the river.

Before the war, Washington was a relatively small city of 61,122 people. During the war, however, it swells with soldiers stationed here to guard it. The city looks like an armed camp. Soldiers patrol bridges and streets. Many schools and churches are turned into hospitals for the wounded. In 1861 a bakery set up at the Capitol turns out sixteen thousand loaves of bread each day for the soldiers.

(Facing page) *Construction workers add the finishing touches to the Capitol building in Washington, D.C.*

POINTS OF INTEREST IN CIVIL WAR AMERICA

0   100   200 in miles

0   100   200

in kilometers

New York City, **NEW YORK**

Pittsburgh, **PENNSYLVANIA**

Gettysburg, **PENNSYLVANIA**

ATLANTIC OCEAN

potomac RIVER

Washington, D.C. ★

Rappahannock River

Appomattox Court House, **VIRGINIA** •

Richmond, **VIRGINIA** ★

City Point, **VIRGINIA**

Hampton Roads, **VIRGINIA**

Charleston, **SOUTH CAROLINA** •

Washington is a political city. You'll see congressmen, governors, and other important people everywhere. President Lincoln's office is on the second floor of the White House. If you're in that neighborhood, you may catch a glimpse of him. You will see slaves with their masters all over town. Slavery is not abolished in the North until after the war.

RICHMOND, VIRGINIA

Richmond, Virginia, is the capital of the Confederacy. In 1860 only 39,910 people lived in Richmond. Like Washington, Richmond swells with troops during the war. In early 1865, you'll find a bustling city of more than 200,000. Richmond is a hub of the tobacco industry. It has four major tobacco warehouses.

One stop you can't miss in Richmond is the home of Jefferson Davis. On May 29, 1861, he becomes president of the Confederacy. People start calling his house the "Confederate White House."

While you're there, look for a slave named Mary Elizabeth Bowser. Jefferson Davis assumes his slaves can't read or write (laws forbid them to learn). But Mary Elizabeth Bowser reads everything she can get her hands on. She also notices everything that goes on around her—and not because she's nosy. She's a spy. Right under Jefferson Davis's nose, she gathers valuable information about the Confederacy, then gives it to the Union army.

Many Civil War battles take place in Virginia. Most of the wounded are taken to Richmond. In fact, about 60 percent of Confederate wounded are treated here. Every available space has been turned into a makeshift hospital. Townspeople are

Hot Hint

Don't visit Richmond on April 2, 1865. Union forces capture the city that day. Confederate troops set fire to their own tobacco warehouses to keep the Union army from seizing them. The flames leap to nearby houses and shops, and the whole city burns.

Richmond, Virginia, lies in ruins after a massive fire destroys the city.

feeling the war in other ways, too. In March 1865, a Richmond newspaper declares that bakeries are selling loaves of bread barely visible to the naked eye.

CHICAGO, ILLINOIS

If you want to avoid war-torn areas, visit Chicago, Illinois. Illinois is too far "out West" to be a battleground. In 1862 Chicago has about 120,000 residents. Although people here feel somewhat removed from the war, many men have left for the front lines.

Cities along the East Coast are hard hit by the war. But cities such as Chicago are benefiting from it. The Union army desperately needs food, so farmers near Chicago raise prices on their crops. The city's economy booms along with the boom in farm prices.

As you tour Chicago, you'll hear the ringing of the courthouse bell. Rung several times each day, the bell tells people when to get up, when to eat dinner, and when to leave work. The bell is also rung at times of celebration. It rings after Union victories in battles, such as those at Vicksburg, Mississippi, and Gettysburg, Pennsylvania. It also rings when Richmond falls to the Union.

You may be in Chicago when a regiment of soldiers is leaving for the front. People crowd the sidewalks to see the troops march by. Everybody cheers. Some women wave their handkerchiefs in farewell. If the day is hot, people offer ice water or lemonade to the soldiers. They hold out cups the way modern onlookers offer water to runners at a marathon.

MONEY MATTERS

U.S. stamps like these are used as a form of cash in Union military camps.

A POSTAGE STAMP FOR YOUR THOUGHTS

During the Civil War, the U.S. government issues paper money for the first time. The bills are printed with green ink, which is easy to get and resists wear. The green bills are called "greenbacks." You'll see a number such as 5 printed on each greenback. But a 5 doesn't mean the bill is worth five dollars. It's worth five cents.

Silver coins are scarce. So postage stamps are also used as currency during the war. Men leaving for the front lines often take stamps with them as spending money.

If you visit a Union army camp, you'll buy things from sutlers (people who sell goods to soldiers in the camps). Have cash handy, because

A Union one-dollar bill (left) *and a Confederate five-dollar bill* (right)

sutlers don't take American Express. Soldiers can pay by signing a pay voucher. The voucher lets the sutler claim the soldier's army pay. Prices are high, especially if only one sutler is in camp. But at least soldiers can get boots, writing paper, butter, sardines, cheese, fruit, oysters, and many other items.

Back TO THE FUTURE

The first national income tax in the United States begins in 1861. The tax helps the North pay for the war. It applies only to people who make more than one thousand dollars a year. These people have to pay 5 percent of their income. The tax affects few people (no more than 1 percent). But you'll still hear many complaints about it.

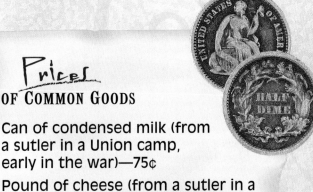

Prices

OF COMMON GOODS

Can of condensed milk (from a sutler in a Union camp, early in the war)—75¢

Pound of cheese (from a sutler in a Union camp, early in the war)—50¢

Pound of butter (from a sutler in a Union camp, early in the war)—$1

Pound of butter (in Confederate dollars, 1864)—$20

MONEY TROUBLES

The Confederate government prints one billion dollars' worth of bills. But it never declares this money as its legal currency. Southern patriotism gives the money temporary value. After the war, it will be worthless.

Shortages in the South cause prices to skyrocket. In 1861 the average family in Richmond spends $6.65 (in Confederate dollars) on food each week. Two years later, the cost is $68.25. By 1864 prices are even higher. You'll need $5 to buy a cup of coffee and $50 for one chicken. Locals joke that innkeepers charge for a night's stay the next morning—in case the price goes up during the night.

SALARIES

Union soldier—$13 to $16 a month (beware: payments are seldom on time)

Confederate soldier—$20 a month (Confederate money)

Teacher—$1 to $2 a month per student

Doctor—25¢ to $2 per visit, plus 50¢ a mile (for the doctor to come to your house)

HOW TO GET AROUND

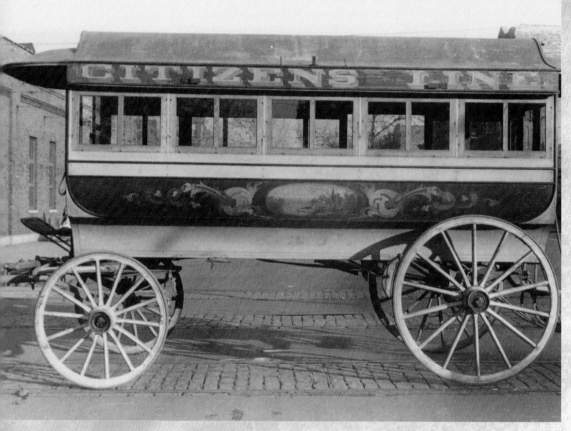

This horse-drawn omnibus transports citizens of Chicago around the city.

BY LAND

Traffic is surprisingly bad in the big cities, especially in the North. You'll be jostled about among hundreds of horse-drawn vehicles. Many streets are often paved with cobblestones. The unevenness makes travel a teeth-rattling experience.

Public transportation is fairly good. You can ride in a variety of vehicles. A cab is a coach, pulled by a horse, that carries one or two passengers. A hack is larger. It holds up to six passengers and is pulled by two horses. The omnibus, or stage, holds twelve passengers. Omnibuses are cheap to ride, but they are very uncomfortable. They are stuffy. And you'll sit on a hard unpadded bench as you rattle along at three to four miles an hour. Look for "horsecars," or horse-drawn trolleys. They are larger, cheaper, and faster than omnibuses. Since they roll along steel rails, they are more comfortable, too.

In the country, many roads aren't paved. You'll find them dusty or muddy, depending on the weather. When thousands of men and horses march from battle to battle, a road gets beaten up even more. New railroad lines crisscross the nation, making it possible to reach many places by rail. You may prefer the train for traveling long distances.

BY WATER

You may find it difficult to travel by water during the war. Before the war, steamboats carried goods up and down rivers such as the Mississippi and the Ohio. People traveled on river steamboats for both pleasure and business. During the war, however, most steamboats are being used to transport troops and army supplies. A few are used as hospital ships.

A medical supply boat docks at Appomattox Landing in Virginia.

If you are in City Point, Virginia, in March 1865, check the harbor for the *River Queen*. This ship serves as a floating headquarters for Union general Ulysses S. Grant. President Lincoln, General Grant, and other top commanders plot their final campaign against the Confederacy aboard this ship.

You'll also find other types of boats being used in the war effort. The North's blockade is a massive job. The Union navy patrols 3,500 miles of coastline. It guards every Confederate harbor. It watches rivers so ships can't sail into river ports. Nearly any boat that can float is called into service. Naval vessels, ferryboats, steamboats, whalers, tugboats, and fishing boats all join to keep the blockade going until the end of the war.

If you visit the West, you'll see pioneers traveling by both land and water. Many travel in wagon trains. Some travel by train. Some pioneers settle along rivers and near railroad lines. Others continue all the way to the West Coast.

LOCAL CUSTOMS & MANNERS

Women in the Soldier's Aid Society of Springfield, Illinois, display handmade goods for Union troops.

WHAT YOU CAN EXPECT FROM CIVILIANS

You'll notice one thing right away about civilians in both the North and the South. They do as much as they can to help the soldiers. Women stitch flags or sew underwear for soldiers. (You'll hear lots of giggling during that last activity.) Girls knit socks to send to their fathers. Boys take on extra chores.

These potholders are for sale at the Chicago Sanitary Fair in 1865. Proceeds go to help soldiers and their families.

Many women belong to groups that help with the war effort. The biggest one in the North is the United States Sanitary Commission. Volunteers help care for wounded soldiers and work for better conditions in army camps and hospitals. You may come upon a "sanitary fair" during your travels. These fairs raise money by selling pies, quilts, jellies, and other items.

In the South, where fighting is most common, charity is very personal. For example, people often offer their own homes as a place to care for wounded soldiers. Many women volunteer as nurses.

Since most men are away at the war, women run the plantations and farms. They also cook and clean. They wash dishes and clothes, shop for

TAKE IT from a Local

I hate weary days of inaction. Yet what can women do but wait and suffer?

—*Kate Stone, writing in her journal after her brothers leave to join the Confederate army*

32

groceries, and empty chamber pots (containers used as toilets during the night). Although busy, many women feel restless. They must carry on with routine life when they would rather help more directly with the war effort.

Some women have jobs outside the home. They teach, work in factories or mills, or do other "women's work." Some want to work, but others have to work to support their families. Many of these women have been widowed by the war.

Wealthy women rarely work. They have servants or slaves to do the housework. Many wealthy women volunteer for charity work. They also call on friends and participate in clubs. Wealthy women change clothes many times each day. That way they're always wearing the right outfit for these social occasions.

BEING A KID

For children in Civil War America, the day's chores begin before the sun comes up. There is no running water or electricity to heat homes.

Women in Lynn, Massachusetts, work in a shoe factory during the Civil War.

So children carry water and fetch wood for the fire. Even the littlest children help.

About half of all kids here go to school. In farm areas, kids generally go to school only between December and March. The rest of the year, they have to help in the fields. In cities, children from poor families often work in factories or mills instead of going to school. Some children attend school at night, after the day's work is done.

If you visit a local school, you'll have no trouble finding your class. Most schools have just one room. A one-room school usually has students from age six to age twenty. If you visit in winter, get a seat near the middle of the room, close to the stove that heats the room. Don't expect a comfortable chair. In some schools, you'll have to make do with a hard plank bench. You'll write with chalk on a slate board about the size of a book.

Expect few, if any, discipline problems. On the first day, the teacher generally gives the class a long list of rules. He or she then points out the yardstick or leather strap used for hitting pupils who don't obey the rules.

Now Hear This

If one Confederate soldier can whip 7 Yankees, how many soldiers can whip 49 Yankees?

—*a problem from* Johnson's Elementary Arithmetic, *a math book used in Raleigh, North Carolina, during the Civil War*

A student may tell you that you've arrived on "potato day" or "onion day." These days have nothing to do with the cafeteria (there isn't one). To help feed the army, schools collect produce from farm families on these days.

FROM DAWN TO DUSK IN THE ARMY

When you first arrive at an army camp, a supply sergeant will issue some equipment to you. You'll carry your own things, so you'll get a knapsack (also called a haver-sack). You'll do most of your own cooking, too (no cafeterias here). So you'll probably get a frying pan, a tin cup, eating utensils, and a canteen. Other supplies may include extra clothes, a sewing kit, a ground cloth that has been oiled to make it water-proof, two wool blankets, a

Several grades are grouped together in this one-room schoolhouse (facing page). A canteen (right) is an important item issued to soldiers when they join the army. You can get mighty thirsty on those marches.

A knapsack (left) *and sewing kit* (right) *are also issued to soldiers. Many soldiers carry* journals (center) *to record day-to-day events.*

gun, and ammunition. You may want to add some personal items such as a journal or paper for writing letters.

Once you've packed all this, your knapsack will be heavy (fifteen to twenty-five pounds). Many soldiers tire of carrying so much weight. They discard the least essential items as they march along. Remember that your gun is essential. Your wool blanket might not be, depending on the weather.

Hot Hint

A soldier may say you've been cheated because you weren't issued an umbrella. He may even insist that you demand one from the supply sergeant. Don't fall for this trick, often played on new recruits. A soldier's equipment does not include an umbrella.

Army life is made up of long stretches of boredom interrupted by brief periods of terror. You will march to battles, but most days you won't. For every one day in battle, you'll spend fifty days in camp.

Camp life begins at dawn. You'll be roused from sleep by a bugle call. After roll call (which is sort of like taking attendance), you'll get dressed and eat breakfast. You'll hear another bugle call. Ignore it unless you have a medical problem—that's the sick call. Clean your area, chop firewood, get water, or do anything else a superior officer orders you to do.

At about 8:00 A.M., you'll join the rest of the soldiers for drill, bayonet practice, or other exercises until lunch. Soldiers call this meal "roast beef" even though the food will not in any way resemble that delicacy. At 4:00 P.M., you'll report for evening parade. Evening parade is not as much fun as it sounds. It's just a march in front of the commanding officers so that they can inspect you.

After supper comes free time and another roll call just before dark. Bedtime is 10:30 P.M. You'll know it's time for bed when you hear the buglers playing "taps."

Confederate soldiers of Company K, Georgia Volunteer Infantry, stand at attention.

Sometimes entire families join a soldier in camp.

Sometimes women (not the ones disguised as men) join their husbands in army camps. Soldiers see few women in camp. So a woman may cause quite a commotion. If you're female and you visit a camp, you may feel more like a film star than a tourist.

You'll probably be frightened if you have to enter battle. But remember that your fellow soldiers are scared, too. One soldier was seen racing away from a battle near Atlanta, Georgia. When asked why he was running, he said, "Because I can't fly."

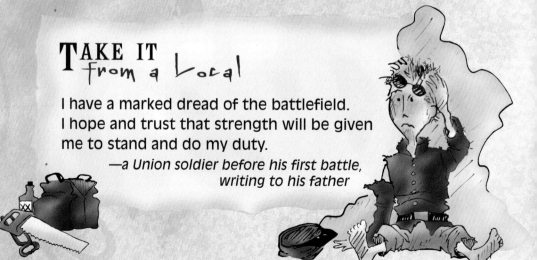

TAKE IT from a Local

I have a marked dread of the battlefield. I hope and trust that strength will be given me to stand and do my duty.

—*a Union soldier before his first battle, writing to his father*

During a battle, you may find it hard to figure out what's going on. Usually the soldiers aren't massed in one place. Instead, small groups are scattered over several miles. Here and there you'll see batteries of large guns. Often the troops are hidden in clouds of smoke. The variety of uniforms (and lack of uniforms) adds to the confusion. On dark nights, you'll find it even harder to see soldiers. But you will see shells flashing through the sky like fireworks.

LOCAL MANNERS

Table manners in an army camp are pretty rough. But even in private homes, you don't need to worry too much about table manners (unless you're attending a formal dinner). People don't wait for food to be passed. They either yell for it or just grab it. You'll see people eating directly from their knives. They cool their coffee or tea by pouring a little into the saucer and then drinking it.

If you visit with a family in a living room, your manners can be informal. You will need your best manners, however, when visiting in the

Soldiers in Maryland enjoy a meal at a makeshift table.

parlor. Expressions such as "O my!" and "O mercy!" are considered rude. Take care not to brag. And avoid religious or moral subjects. These topics can spark tempers, just as they do at home.

LOCAL BELIEFS

You'll find churches wherever you go. Only about half of the locals go to church every week. But most consider themselves Christians. They believe that God controls everything in their lives—from small things to big, important things like the war. Both Northerners and Southerners believe that God is on their side.

The Civil War has divided some churches. Instead of having one national church organization, they have split into Northern and Southern groups.

TAKE IT from a Local

The prayers of both could not be answered.
—*Abraham Lincoln, commenting on the outcome of the Civil War*

On Sunday mornings, churchgoers dress in their best clothes to go to church. Later they visit relatives, nap, read, or write letters. Some attend a short evening church service. Sunday is a day of rest for everyone, so don't expect stores to be open. People cook their meals for Sunday on Saturday. Servants usually have the day off.

Out in the country, you may meet a circuit rider (traveling preacher). Circuit riders travel on horseback between towns that are too small to have their own preacher. They lead church services, weddings, and funerals. An ambitious circuit rider may do three sermons in one day.

A priest conducts church services for soldiers in a military camp.

Circuit riders stay in people's homes, so you may find yourself sharing a room with one. Sometimes a circuit rider stays with a family for a week or more. The preacher makes himself useful, helping with the chores.

DEATH & BEYOND

With luck you won't need to understand burial customs here. But if someone you meet does die, you may be invited to the funeral. The family of the deceased will notify you in writing. They often use stationery with a black border.

To prepare someone for burial, the family washes and dresses the body. They do not have it embalmed (preserved with chemicals) unless it must be shipped a long way. Then they lay the body out, usually in the parlor. Friends and relatives come to view the dead person. When you arrive, you should comment on how natural or peaceful the person looks.

Coffins tend to be simple wooden boxes. In some cities, ornate caskets are available to people who can afford them. These are made from metal or hard woods that protect loved ones from worms.

Usually the coffin rests on a board with blocks of ice underneath. The ice helps to preserve the body until the funeral. The family may put flowers in the room to mask unpleasant odors. One clever invention is called a "corpse cooler." It contains ice and keeps the body fresher longer.

Funeral ceremonies vary. Just as in modern times, the type depends on the area of the country and on the person's religion. The service will likely be held in the dead person's home. You'll notice a black wreath or ribbon on the front door.

Don't worry about wearing black. Most locals just wear their church clothes. They believe that death is just a passage from one life to the next. A funeral shouldn't be overly gloomy. A minister will read from the Bible, say a few prayers, and talk about the person's good qualities. Some people hold a second service at the graveside.

You are more likely to see a funeral if you witness a battle. It is impossible to prepare yourself for the horrors of this terrible war. A visit to a battlefield is definitely not for the squeamish.

Soldiers worry not only about dying but also about their families. Unlike modern soldiers, they carry no dog tags or other forms of identification. If they die, their bodies might never be identified. Then their

families will never know what became of them. Soldiers also fear bringing shame on themselves and their families. That could happen if, under fire, they prove to be cowards and run away.

For the men who die in battle, the usual funeral traditions do not apply. A soldier's coffin may be no more than a blanket or a sack.

TAKE IT from a Local

Death is nothing here. As you step out in the morning from your tent to wash your face, you see before you on a stretcher a shapeless, extended object, and over it is thrown a dark gray blanket. It is the corpse of some wounded or sick soldier of the regiment who died in the hospital tent during the night.
—*poet Walt Whitman*

Men prepare graves for fellow soldiers. Some of the dead will be buried in pine boxes, while others are buried in nothing but a blanket.

43

WHAT TO WEAR

SOLDIERS' UNIFORMS

You may have heard about the "blues and grays." Sometimes Union soldiers do wear blue uniforms and Confederate soldiers wear gray. But sometimes the reverse is true. Some Confederate regiments wear blue (or brown). Some Union regiments wear gray. Western regiments may wear buckskin uniforms. The men of the 79th New York Highlanders wear kilts. The result is often confusion about who is who.

If you are traveling as a soldier, you'll get a full uniform when you enlist. Uniforms come in two sizes: too big and too small. Try trading with someone else to get one close to your size. If you're in the Union army, your uniform is wool. (You've never really been hot until you've marched in a wool uniform . . . in the summer . . . in the South.)

You'll also be given a necktie and drawers (ankle-length underwear). Many men don't wear the necktie. Men from the rural South also skip the drawers. After marching a few hours, though, a soldier's skin chafes against the rough fabric of his trousers. A word to the wise: wear your drawers.

Hot Hint

Try to get a uniform that is a little big. It will shrink after it gets wet, as it probably will the first time it rains.

(Facing page) *Cadet Thomas Garland Jefferson wears an ill-fitting uniform.*

A pair of soldier's shoes looks worn from years of use.

Because of the North's blockade, clothes are scarce in the South. And the longer the war goes on, the harder it is to get uniforms or every-day clothes. So some Southern troops don't have uniforms. They wear civilian clothes. As their uniforms or other clothes wear out, soldiers wear whatever they can find. They even take uniforms from dead Union soldiers.

If you find sturdy shoes even remotely close to your size, grab them. In both the North and the South, good shoes are scarce. Most are cheaply made and fall apart quickly. Southern soldiers often go barefoot. Two battles—Antietam and Gettysburg—resulted, at least in part, from the Southern army's search for shoes. Long marches mean you're almost sure to get painful blisters and sores, even with good shoes.

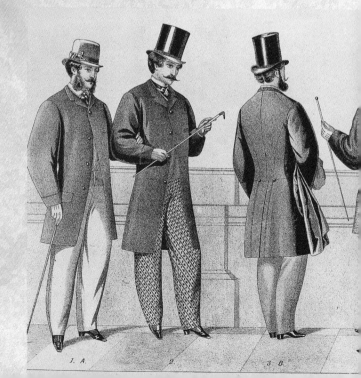

The hottest men's fashions for 1865 are shown here in an ad for Broadway Fashions, New York.

CLOTHES FOR MEN

Fabric shortages make it hard to replace clothes as they wear out. Clothes are mended or turned inside out to extend their wear. People aren't used to spinning their own wool and linen, since factories make cloth. But some people bring their spinning wheels out of storage and begin spinning their own fabrics again.

Men's clothes aren't that different from what you see at home. Businessmen wear suits. Shirts (usually white) are loose-fitting. Collars and cuffs are starched stiff. Pants are a bit baggier, and they're held up with suspenders instead of belts. A man without a hat would be odd. So if you're male, wear a top hat, felt hat, straw hat, or rounded bowler.

Some working men wear a new kind of pants first used by miners during the California gold rush of the 1850s. You may not recognize the sturdy brown fabric. But you do know the name of the company that makes the pants—Levi Strauss.

Don't expect the many shoe options you have at home. You won't get a perfect fit, since sizes are limited. Shoes for both feet are shaped the same.

Men and children wear high-top shoes fastened with laces or buttons. There are no cross-trainers, but you may notice the first sneakers. These rubber-soled shoes are worn for "extreme" sports such as croquet and archery. Farmers wear heavy work shoes. Many other country people go barefoot. They see shoes as something a person wears to dress up.

After the North begins its blockade, shoe choices are severely limited in the South. Most families start tanning their own leather and making their own shoes. Toward the end of the war, sturdy shoes are all sent to the front lines. People make do with shoes made of cloth or even paper.

CLOTHES FOR WOMEN

Women's clothes are more varied than men's. In the country, you'll need just two or three floor-length dresses. The long skirts and sleeves on your dress will hide your ankles and arms. Most dresses are made of linsey-woolsey (a blend of linen and wool) or of colorful cottons such as calico and gingham. Save the nicest dress for Sundays and for special occasions.

City women are more fashion conscious. They

This girl's jewelry and the elaborate trim on her dress show that she is wearing her Sunday best.

Hoops and crinolines hold this well-dressed woman's skirt in a bell shape.

wear frilly, decorated hats. Their dresses have wide skirts that balloon out elegantly from a tiny waist. Women wear several layers of petticoats under their skirts. Look for them in rich colors. Some petticoats have scallops, beautiful embroidery, or other fancy trim.

The bad news, if you're female, is that you'll be uncomfortable. To make your waist tiny, you'll need a corset (a kind of girdle around your middle). You may find it hard to breathe. To hold your skirt wide, you'll wear an uncomfortable hoop or cage. Or you may wear crinolines (petticoats made of linen and horsehair). They are so stiff you won't need a hoop.

IMPORTANT
Safety Tip

It's possible to get stuck in a doorway in your huge, crinoline-puffed skirt. It's so wide that it can easily sweep too close to a stove or fireplace. You could go up in flames if you aren't careful!

IMPORTANT

Safety Tip

If you have acne, beware the popular local treatment Fowler's Solution. It contains arsenic, which can be deadly.

You won't find the many beauty products you see at home. But women do experiment with perfumes and wear rouge. You'll find some skin care products but no sunblock. A tan is considered coarse. (Only a person who works outside in the fields would be tan!) So you'll need a sunbonnet when you go outdoors.

HAIR

Women, especially in cities, take great care of their hair. They wash it (this alone is an improvement over earlier days), and they also style it elaborately. Most pull it back into a "waterfall" of long curls. If your hair isn't long enough, you can wear a horsehair hairpiece to get the same effect.

Men wear an astonishing array of beards, mustaches, and sideburns. (Even President Lincoln recently grew a beard.) Hair on the face is considered handsome. Some men do shave, but even they shave only every other day.

A Civil War–era men's hygiene kit contains a bar of soap, a brush, a razor, and a comb.

WHAT TO SEE & DO

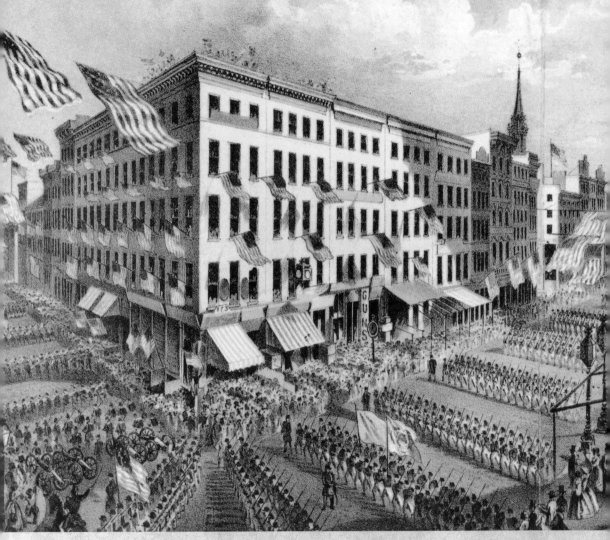

If you can, be sure to see soldiers on their way to battle.

SOLDIERS ON THE MOVE

A procession of soldiers marching (to a new place—not into battle) is an inspiring sight. The procession is usually led by a band of drummers, buglers, and other musicians playing patriotic songs and other tunes.

Battle wages between the Monitor *(left) and the* Merrimac *(right). The* Merrimac *is a sunken wooden ship raised by the Confederates, plated in iron, and renamed the* Virginia. *Most folks continue to call it the* Merrimac, *though.*

Next come the top commanders. The officers follow, each leading a company of soldiers. Bringing up the rear are supply wagons, laborers (often African Americans), and a rear guard. One procession worth watching is the troops heading out of Washington, D.C., on July 16, 1861. They are on their way to Manassas, Virginia, for the first major battle of the war.

Hot Hint

At Bull Run, T. J. Jackson, a Union general, inspires his men to stand their ground despite the fierce attack of the Confederates. Another general points out Jackson, exclaiming, "There is Jackson standing like a stone wall!" The nickname "Stonewall" Jackson sticks.

THE BATTLE OF BULL RUN

One battle you may want to see happens near Washington, D.C., on July 21, 1861. You can join other people in Washington, who pack picnic lunches and drive their carriages to the site of the Battle of Bull Run. Then they watch the battle from a safe distance.

You'll notice that the Confederates are winning. Try to leave the scene before mid-afternoon. The Union troops start to flee back to Washington. Most onlookers stay too long and have to retreat at the same time. Carriages, soldiers, and army wagons all get stuck in a giant traffic jam. The jam becomes a crisis when a Confederate shell explodes near the road, overturning a wagon and blocking the way out. Eventually, most onlookers do return to Washington alive.

THE *MONITOR* & THE *MERRIMAC*

Another interesting battle is between two ships, the *Monitor* and the *Merrimac*. Their fight is the first ever between ironclad ships (ships with iron hulls). You can see the battle from the shore at Hampton Roads, Virginia, on Saturday, March 8, 1862.

That day, the *Merrimac,* a Confederate ship, attacks weaker Union ships in the harbor at Hampton Roads. The Union men are hanging out their laundry to dry when the attack begins. The next day, the *Monitor* suddenly appears and opens fire on the *Merrimac*. The *Monitor* looks funny (it is often called a "cheese box on a raft"), and it has only two guns, while the *Merrimac* has eight. But the *Monitor* is better armored and is the stronger ship. It circles the *Merrimac,* firing on weak spots.

Eventually the *Monitor* damages the *Merrimac,* which retreats. This battle signals the end of the era of wooden ships.

THE BATTLE FOR FORT WAGNER

Fort Wagner is a Confederate stronghold. It stands at the entrance to the harbor of Charleston, South Carolina. The job of capturing the fort for the Union falls to the Massachusetts 54th, an African American regiment formed in 1863. Colonel Robert Gould Shaw, a white officer, commands the regiment.

On July 18, 1863, the men of the Massachusetts 54th storm Fort Wagner. More troops are promised, but they never come. The regiment fights bravely. They get inside the fort and disable its big guns. But they are outnumbered and cannot capture the fort. Shaw is killed.

The Massachusetts 54th loses its battle. The story of their courage spreads, however, and many Northerners change their attitudes toward African Americans. This battle paves the way for more African Americans to become soldiers. By October 1864, more than one hundred thousand black soldiers are fighting in 140 black regiments. By the end of the war, 15 percent of the Union forces are African American, as are forty-three hundred casualties.

African Americans who serve as Union soldiers suffer more hardships than other soldiers. They get inferior equipment, harsher treatment, poorer food, and less pay. They are more likely to be sent into especially dangerous battles and difficult areas, such as swamps.

Back TO THE FUTURE

Twenty-three soldiers from the Massachusetts 54th eventually receive Congressional Medals of Honor. In 1989 an Oscar-winning film, *Glory*, tells this regiment's story.

The Massachusetts 54th regiment attacks Confederate troops at Fort Wagner.

Like other Union soldiers, black soldiers are sometimes captured by the Confederates. But they face a worse fate than other Union soldiers. By Confederate law, any African American caught with a weapon is put to death.

THE GETTYSBURG ADDRESS

Try to get to Gettysburg, Pennsylvania, on November 19, 1863. A local cemetery is being dedicated as a national burial ground for soldiers. Arrive well before 10:00 A.M. to find a good spot to stand among the fifteen thousand spectators. Edward Everett, a politician, is on the program. Everett is famous for his eloquent speeches. He talks for two hours about the noble deeds of the Union dead.

A photographer is on hand to photograph President Lincoln. When Lincoln begins to speak, the photographer starts to get ready. Camera equipment in this era is cumbersome. Lincoln's speech is short, about three hundred words. It takes him less than three minutes. By the time the photographer is ready, Lincoln is finished speaking.

People in the audience are not impressed with Lincoln's Gettysburg Address. Local people expect long, flowery speeches. But Edward Everett understands the power of Lincoln's few words. He tells Lincoln, "I would be glad if I could flatter myself that I came as near the central idea of the occasion in two hours, as you did in two minutes."

Now Hear This

Four score and seven years ago our fathers brought forth, upon this continent, a new nation, conceived in Liberty, and dedicated to the proposition that all men are created equal.
—*Abraham Lincoln, the opening sentence of the* Gettysburg Address

THE SURRENDER OF THE SOUTH

If you want to see an important historic moment, join Confederate general Robert E. Lee and Union general Ulysses S. Grant on April 9, 1865. They sign the terms of surrender for the Civil War on that day. Lee is in full dress uniform, complete with shiny boots and an impressive sword. He has carried the uniform with him throughout the war. Grant is wearing a private's shirt and muddy boots. He doesn't have a sword.

Robert E. Lee (right, with pen) *surrenders to Ulysses S. Grant* (hatless, at left) *at the Appomattox Courthouse in Virginia.*

Nevertheless, Grant is a classy guy. He knows he has brought the South to its knees. But he resists the temptation to gloat. Lee offers his sword to Grant as a token of his personal surrender. But Grant refuses to take it. Grant also lets Confederate officers keep their side arms (weapons worn at the side or in the belt). And he allows Confederate soldiers to keep their horses. Graciously he tells Lee, "Each officer and man will be allowed to return to his home, not to be disturbed by the United States authorities."

After the commanders sign the surrender papers, they salute each other. The war is officially over (although some people do keep fighting). Then Lee goes outside, mounts his horse Traveller, and begins to leave. The victorious Union men waiting outside start firing guns in celebration, but Grant stops them. "We did not want to exult over their downfall," he explains later.

Notice the twenty thousand or so Confederate troops lining the road. They have struck their tents (taken them down) and prepared to go home. Barefoot and hungry, they know their side has lost, but many beg Lee to tell them it isn't so.

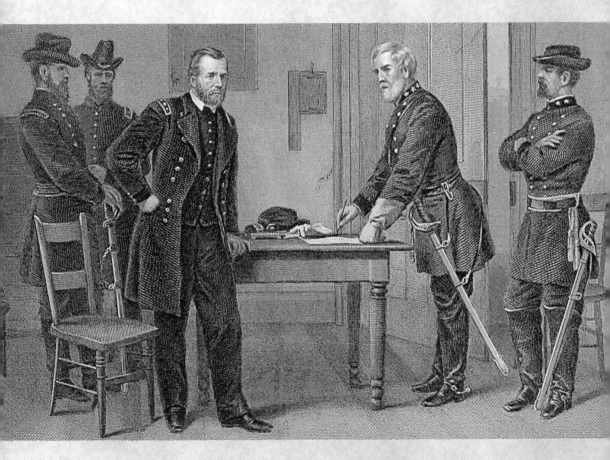

A Southern family prepares for a game of croquet.

WHERE TO FIND SPORTS & RECREATION

GAMES

If you stay with an ordinary family, you'll find that the children and parents gather in the evenings to share quiet activities. They read, sew, and write letters. Children also do homework, of course.

Some evening pastimes are more lively. Some families stage their own magic or puppet shows. Games such as checkers, charades, and twenty questions are popular. You'll hardly miss the Internet. Honest.

One of the most popular outdoor games is croquet. You may have played croquet (you hit a ball with a mallet through little arches called wickets). Croquet is so popular that some manufacturers put candleholders on the wickets so people can play after dark.

Don't play "Pop Goes the Canteen" while visiting an army camp. In this game, a soldier fills a canteen with gunpowder, corks it, and tosses it into the campfire. The canteen then explodes. Obviously people can get hurt. In addition, the commotion might make the men think they are under attack. When the real cause is uncovered, the culprit may be in for a thrashing. The noise could also attract nearby enemy troops.

SPORTS

You'll enjoy some delightful sports if you travel with the army. Olympic athletes don't enter greased pig competitions, but Civil War soldiers do. To join the fun, you try to catch a pig coated with grease to make it slippery.

Baseball is just starting to catch on. Many people use a stick or a fencepost as a bat. The ball is a walnut covered with yarn. The rules are the same as the ones you know. But players aren't as skilled as those you're used to. Their pitching is particularly weak. Final scores tend to be higher, more like a modern football score than a modern baseball score. In one

I M P O R T A N T
Safety Tip

Watch for people loading snowballs with rocks or bullets. This is not uncommon in snowball fights that get out of control. A loaded snowball can cause serious injury.

baseball game between two Union regiments, the 13th Massachusetts and the 104th New York, the final score is 66 to 20. Bet on the Massachusetts team.

Other sports are wrestling, shooting contests (the person with the best aim wins), running races, and tenpins (bowling). Snowball fights are popular in winter. Regiments battle each other, even taking "prisoners of war."

Soldiers team up to play baseball to entertain themselves between battles. Here are examples of baseball equipment and uniforms.

A group of Confederate soldiers passes the time playing dominoes.

RECREATIONAL ACTIVITIES

You may want to read the newspaper while staying in an army camp. If you find one, though, it will probably be a month or more old. Be alert if a horseback rider gallops in with a stack of newspapers. Everyone will rush to get in line the minute they hear the cry "Papers!" In Union camps, expect to pay five cents for a newspaper from Washington or Philadelphia. Newspapers from New York cost twice as much.

Music is the most common entertainment. Many regiments have bands. Some perform concerts for local residents as well as for other soldiers. And if you like to sing, you're in luck. Soldiers sing often, while marching or doing chores. A sing-along during evening campfire is the most fun. You might know some of the songs. Many of them have patriotic themes. "Battle Hymn of the Republic" and "Yankee Doodle" are favorites in the North. A Southern favorite is "God Save the South."

Sometimes one soldier accompanies a sing-along with a harmonica, violin, or banjo. Soldiers sometimes dance to the music. You may even see a mock "ball," with some men dancing the women's parts.

Surprisingly, Union and Confederate troops sometimes sing together. When camped near each other, the men from one side can sometimes hear the distant singing of the other. The two sides may join in one familiar tune, serenading each other in the dark.

Between battles, Union and Confederate troops may also be friendly in other ways. Sometimes the men compete in boxing matches or hold dances. Sometimes they trade supplies (coffee for tobacco, for example).

You might even see a play. Some soldiers organize variety shows or theater productions. These can be quite elaborate. Some are performed in local theaters. Ticket proceeds sometimes go to help injured soldiers or struggling civilians.

WHERE TO STAY

Army camps are far from glamorous. This camp, Fort Sedgewick, is known by soldiers as "Fort Hell."

SOLDIER ACCOMMODATIONS

The roughest housing (except, perhaps, for slave housing) is in the army camps. Camp conditions vary. In the winter, you'll probably stay in a log hut. Or you may use a "bombproof" shelter dug into the ground or built into the side of a hill. You'll sleep on a bunk bed made from boxes, pieces of barrel, or even tree branches. In summer, you might simply sleep on the ground wrapped in blankets. Confederate soldiers are more likely to sleep under the stars than Union soldiers.

TAKE IT from a Local

Now I lay me down to sleep
In mud that's many fathoms deep;
If I'm not here when you awake,
Just hunt me up with an oyster rake.

—*the revised prayer of a soldier on the "Mud March" led by General Ambrose Burnside in January 1863 after a two-day rainstorm*

Tents are a common type of shelter. Expect to feel crowded in a tent. You may have to lie stacked like spoons with five or six other soldiers to fit inside your small tent. This can be unpleasant, since soldiers aren't all that clean. On hot, humid nights, the odor of all those sweaty people may make sleeping difficult.

Some army tents look like tents you'd see at home. But late in the war, you'll probably notice shelter tents (also called "dog tents"). Shared by two people, these small tents are supported at each end by a gun with a bayonet attached.

You may also see tents that look like tepees. Called Sibley tents, these tents each have a center tent pole, which often holds a rack for guns. To sleep, everyone lies around the pole like spokes on a wheel. Put your feet at the center and your head near the outside of the tent.

Union soldiers from New York share this Sibley tent.

A Sibley tent holds ten to twenty men. In chilly weather, it is heated by a little stove.

Candles generally supply the only light in a tent. If you can't find a candlestick, simply take the bayonet off your gun. Stick the sharp end in the ground and put the candle in the loop at the top.

There is no bathroom in an army camp. When you need one, look for the "sink." A sink is simply a shallow, open ditch. Usually it is right next to the tents or other living quarters. Soldiers pretty much go to the bathroom wherever they please, however. Add to this piles of rotting food and other garbage and swarms of flies, maggots, and mosquitoes. Camp isn't exactly a picture-postcard scene.

IMPORTANT
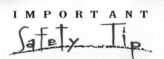

Raise your stove off the ground by placing it on bricks or stones. This keeps your blanket from falling into the fire during the night. You'll also create a warm place under the stove that works as an oven.

PRIVATE HOMES

You'll find a variety of homes in Civil War America. People live in elegant mansions, clapboard houses, and rough dwellings of logs or sod, to name just a few. Others stay in simple boardinghouses and apartments.

If you stay with a middle-class family, you'll probably find yourself in a two-story wood house. On the first floor is a parlor, family room, and dining room. On the second floor are bedrooms, a bathroom (which doesn't have a toilet), and a privy (which does have a toilet). Guests don't venture into the pantry and cellar, since these are considered work areas.

Your host may have furniture made in one of the nation's new factories. Factory-made tables and chairs are much cheaper than those that are handmade. The house will probably also have wallpaper, carpets, and pictures on the wall. Most locals try to match the furnishings in each room rather than have a mishmash of styles. The best furniture and most expensive possessions are showcased in the front parlor, where guests are entertained.

You'll find fireplaces in many of the rooms. But you'll also see some coal- or wood-burning stoves used for heat. A few city homes even have furnaces in the basement that vent warm air into the upper floors.

Don't expect your hosts to have indoor plumbing. In a small privy near the bedrooms, you may find a commode. A commode is a wooden toilet with a metal pail or shaft. More likely you'll use an outdoor privy during the day and a chamber pot at night.

Every drop of clean water has to be carried into the house, and every drop of waste-water has to be carried out. So you'll freshen up in your bedroom, not in a bathroom. You'll find a pitcher of water, a basin, and a towel rack on the washstand. In the cupboard under the washstand, you'll find a footbath and a slop jar (for the dirty water).

Hot Hint

On cold mornings, you may want to dress in the kitchen near the warm stove, as the locals do.

In many homes, people take baths in a tub in the kitchen, basement, or yard. Carrying water takes a lot of effort. You'll probably make do by sponging off using a small bucket of water. If you're lucky, the house where you stay will have a separate bathing room. It is about the size of a closet and has a metal tub about four feet long. Don't get too excited about taking a hot bath, though. The water for the tub generally comes from a holding tank in the attic. You'll have to heat it in the kitchen, then lug it upstairs, bucket by bucket. After you bathe, bail out the bathtub (there is no drain). Remember to carry the wastewater back downstairs.

Speaking of personal hygiene, not everyone here brushes their teeth. If you want to brush yours, you won't find toothpaste, as such, or tooth-brushes. Some people make a paste for their teeth by boiling water, then adding lemon juice, salt, and a powder called burnt alum. They apply this mixture with their fingers, a bit of sponge, or a small brush—take that, bad breath!

A single-story clapboard house in North Carolina

If you stay with a wealthy family, you'll probably sleep on a feather mattress and pillows. Ordinary people are more likely to have mattresses stuffed with cornhusks, straw, or cotton and moss. Don't be surprised to find the windows open at night, even in winter. The locals consider good ventilation (fresh air) essential to good health.

If you are traveling as a Confederate soldier, you'll find many places to stay. During the war, some Southerners who don't usually take in boarders do welcome Confederate soldiers into their homes. The soldiers are treated as honored guests.

PUBLIC ACCOMMODATIONS

Local people as well as travelers often stay in boardinghouses. Many people take boarders into their homes as a way to earn extra money. High-end boardinghouses can be elegant mansions with lavish rooms. On the low end, some landlords simply set up a tent for boarders or rent out a shack.

You will probably rent a single room. Sometimes suites of rooms are available for families. You'll eat meals, which are often included in the cost, with the other boarders. If there is a parlor, you may be invited to use it.

WHAT TO EAT

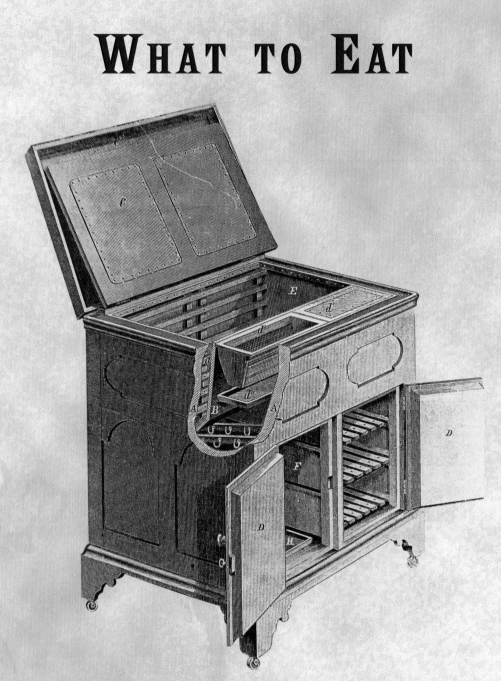

This icebox, called a Bunn's Esquimaux Refrigerator, keeps food cool using blocks of ice cut from nearby lakes in the winter.

COMMON FOODS

Civilians in Civil War America eat hearty breakfasts. They need plenty of food since they face long hours of hard work on the farm or in the city. A breakfast of pork or steak, eggs, fried potatoes, pancakes, coffee, and fruit pies or doughnuts is usual (people haven't discovered choles-terol yet!). You can find porridge (hot cereal) but no cold cereal until the 1870s.

If you stay in a private home, your hosts will serve the main meal, dinner, in the afternoon. You may get turkey, chicken, and in some places, lamb. In the South, you may be offered pork or fried chicken. In the North, beef is preferred. A popular Northern dish is corned beef and cabbage.

Everyone loves potatoes. You'll find them mashed, boiled, baked, fried, and stewed. Southerners prefer sweet potatoes but serve them in the same ways. Other vegetables, when you find them, will generally be overcooked and mushy. Sometimes they're fried in lard. The only popu-lar vegetables are corn, cabbage, tomatoes, and celery.

You'll get plenty of fruit and lots of baked goods. Fruit pies are par-ticularly popular. You will also find biscuits, breads, and cakes. People make all these things themselves. One woman made 421 pies, 152 cakes, 2,140 doughnuts, and 1,038 loaves of bread in one year (and apparently counted them as well!).

If your hosts have food that must be kept cool, they use an icebox. This large wooden box is lined with tin or zinc and is kept cool by a block of ice. The ice is cut in chunks from frozen streams and lakes in winter. Then it's stored in underground icehouses to keep it frozen until it is delivered to homes.

In cities, you'll find plenty of "fast food" (definitely not originated by McDonald's or Burger King). At midday flocks of workers descend on saloons, oyster bars, and other eateries. They bolt down a sizable meal, pay, and leave within ten minutes. (If a store clerk puts out a sign that says "Out for lunch—back in ten minutes," he means it.) A for-eign visitor watching Americans eat this way was reminded of "a piggery at swill-time." Popular foods for lunch include meat and cheese sandwiches, boiled eggs, and pigs' feet. (You won't get fries with that. French fries don't appear until after the war.)

Hot Hint

If you buy a five-cent beer in some restaurants, your meal comes free.

Soldiers can cash in meal tickets for food at the camp's dining hall.

ARMY FARE

If you enjoy fine dining, the army is not for you. The best days are when those camp merchants, sutlers, are around. They offer all kinds of good things to eat. You can get sweets, fresh fruit, butter, cheese, ginger ale, and even canned goods. Their pies are particularly popular and, at twenty-five cents apiece, quite a bargain. No one really knows what is in a sutler's pies, however. Locals joke that these pies are "moist and indigestible below, tough and indestructible above, with untold horrors within."

More often you'll eat regular army food. It is dependably bad. Day after day, you can expect pretty much the same fare. You may eat salt pork or salt beef. Occasionally soldiers also receive potatoes, peas, beans, rice, hominy (dried corn), pepper, and vinegar. Most of the time, though, soldiers get by on coffee and hardtack (hard bread made from flour or cornmeal and water).

Soldiers gather outside a sutler's store, where they can purchase food and other goods.

FOOD TO TRY

- Sutler's pies—pastry items sold by sutlers to soldiers. Although no one will be able to tell you what is in these mysterious little pies, they are very popular.

- Doughnuts—here they have no hole in the middle. The custom of making doughnuts with holes starts toward the end of the 1800s.

Hardtack looks like a thick saltine. It's usually two to three inches across and nearly half an inch thick. Hardtack lasts for weeks or even months, which explains why it's a common food for soldiers on the move.

Eating hardtack may be a shock to you. It's hard enough to be a left-over from, say, the Jurassic Age. If that isn't appetizing enough, hardtack is often filled with burrowing insects called weevils. Soldiers call them "squirmers." A piece of hardtack that is riddled with worms is called a "worm castle." If you are forced to eat after dark, when you can't inspect your hardtack, break it into a cup of boiling coffee, stir it, and pour off the top of the solution. With luck, most of the insects will float away. Some soldiers say the taste of hardtack also improves when they soak it in coffee or fry it in grease. But don't count on it.

If you're lucky, your regiment may find and slaughter a pig or other animal. But soldiers don't usually get fresh meat. Instead they eat salted meat. Salted meat has to be rinsed well before cooking. Otherwise it tastes too salty. Soldiers sometimes soak salted meat in a stream

TAKE IT from a Local

Hardtack . . . was positively unsuitable food for anything that claims to be human.

—*Private Wilbur Fisk of the 2nd Vermont*

Hot Hint

The Union blockade stops salt (essential for preserving meat) from reaching the Confederacy. So Southerners start making their own salt. Union forces then target these salt works. The resulting salt shortage contributes to the defeat of the Confederacy.

overnight by tying it to a rope and letting it float. This allows the meat to "freshen." You can decide how "fresh" your salt beef is when you smell it boiling. It gives off a thoroughly revolting odor.

Don't be surprised if the day's meat is spoiled. If it is spectacularly bad, soldiers may amuse themselves by holding a funeral for it. They put it in a coffin and assign pallbearers to carry it. An old harness is displayed as a symbol that the meat tastes more like horse than beef. Solemn music, mourners, and a gun salute fired over the "grave" complete this stately affair.

If you like to play with your food, try the vegetables. Soldiers call them "desiccated vegetables." This ration is just as tasty as it sounds. Scraps of unidentifiable vegetables are pressed into a little cube and dried (one local thought perhaps in a pottery kiln). One cube weighs about an ounce, but it swells to an astonishing size when soaked in water.

If you've heard hospital food at home is bad, you should see Civil War hospital food. Author Louisa May Alcott (who will later write the book *Little Women*) works as a nurse in a Civil War hospital. She reports that the three meals consist of "beef, evidently put down for the men of '76 [1776!]; pork, just in from the street; army bread, composed of sawdust and saleratus [a substance like baking soda]; butter; salt as if churned by Lot's wife; stewed blackberries, so much like preserved cockroaches, that only those devoid of imagination could partake thereof with relish; coffee, mild and muddy; tea, three dried huckleberry leaves to a quart of water—flavored with lime—also animated and unconscious of any approach to clearness."

If you travel with Confederate troops, you'll find the food even worse than in the Union army. Instead of vegetables, you may get burned wheat and chicory. You may have to forage as you march. Foraging soldiers pocket acorns, green apples, and potato vines as snacks.

Some Confederate soldiers look forward to battle since they may find food in the sacks of fallen Union soldiers. You may even find yourself stealing from the horses' rations to avoid starving. One Confederate regiment kills and eats its own mules in order to stay alive.

WOULD YOU CARE FOR COFFEE WITH THAT?

The coffee you get in the army will not be brewed and served in a handy paper cup. Instead, you'll be given coffee beans. Crush them with a rock or the butt of your gun. Fill your tin cup with the smashed beans and some water and set it in the campfire to boil. Soldiers rarely get sugar for their coffee—and never milk.

If you travel to the South after 1862, your "coffee" is likely to be made from parched rye, parched wheat, or even sweet potatoes or corn. This wonderful beverage is known as "Confederate coffee." Drink if only it you are really desperate.

You can also use sweet potato coffee another way. The sediment in the bottom will remove stains in rugs or carpets. This should tell you something about how it tastes.

FOODS TO TRY, at your own risk

- Bully soup—hot cereal made from cornmeal and hardtack, boiled in water, wine, and ginger

- Skillygalee—hardtack soaked in water and then fried in pork grease (popular among Union troops). The locals say skillygalee makes the hair curl.

- Confederate champagne—three parts water and one part each corn and molasses, fermented in an old molasses barrel

73

WHERE TO FIND SOUVENIRS

Mathew Brady (center) *travels with his picture gallery throughout the Civil War, photographing scenes from battlefields and army camps.*

ARTS, CRAFTS, & OTHER DELIGHTS

A terrific souvenir, if you can manage it, is a photograph by Mathew Brady. Brady is known for his photographs of important Civil War battles. He also photographs scenes in army camps.

Brady runs portrait galleries in Washington, D.C., and in New York City. You'll find the New York gallery at 359 Broadway. It's decorated with chandeliers and velvet tapestries. Brady may be willing to let you pose for him.

President Abraham Lincoln posed for Brady in the Washington gallery. Brady had the portrait printed on cards. One of these cards would be a great memento. Hundreds of thousands are being sold in bookstores, saloons, and general stores.

Brady often travels with the Union army. He uses a portable dark-room (locals call it a "What's it Wagon"). Brady also employs a number of other photographers. He sends them to various battlefields. His goal is to document as much of the war as possible.

Many of Brady's battlefield scenes are gruesome. When he displays the photographs in New York City, the scenes shock people. A reporter writes that the photographs "bring home to us the terrible reality... of war."

Another neat souvenir would be a brass twelve-pounder (a type of cannon). Twelve-pounders have the name of the manufacturer stamped on the barrel. Try to get one stamped "Revere Copper Co., Canton, Mass." This company is owned by descendants of Paul Revere (the famous patriot of the American Revolution).

If you like unusual toys, shop for a toy inspired by the war. "Running the Blockade" is a board game. The object of the game is for players to make it safely through a maze of enemy ships and other hazards to reach safe harbor. Toy soldiers are plentiful. Some soldiers are mechanical toys. One group of wooden soldiers on a board marches when you pull a lever.

THE GENERAL STORE

If you're in a small town, the best place to find a souvenir is the general store. Inside you'll smell pickles, peppermint, coffee, and kerosene. Goods such as flour are stored in waist-high barrels on the floor. Shelves on every wall display a huge variety of merchandise.

With so many options, choosing one souvenir might be a little over-whelming. You'll find practical things, such as fishhooks, wagon wheels, and chamber pots, that no local would go without. The store also stocks items that aren't necessary but are desirable, such as hats, suspenders, and sardines. Sheer luxuries include candy, whisky, and perfume. You can buy a plow, too, but it won't fit into your suitcase.

While you're at the general store, visit with some of the town folk. The general store is where they hang out. They gossip, grab a bite to eat, and shop. They might even pick up the mail, since general stores often serve as a town's post office.

BEST BUYS

Confederate stamps—stamps issued by the Southern Post Office. These will cost you only three to ten cents. At home they are worth one thousand dollars or more apiece as collector's items.

Union currency—particularly paper money in denominations of three, five, or ten cents

Decks of cards—especially handmade decks

How to Stay Safe & Healthy

An ambulance crew demonstrates how it removes wounded soldiers from the battlefield.

Take Some Jimsonweed & Call Me in the Morning

Battles are a serious threat to health in Civil War America. Army surgeons find it almost impossible to treat the massive numbers of soldiers wounded in large battles. Wounded men often lie for days in the fields where they fall. Many die before help reaches them.

In the wagons were men wounded and mutilated in every conceivable way. Some had their legs shattered by a shell or minnie ball; some were shot through their bodies; others had arms torn to shreds; some had received a ball in the face. . . .

—*Confederate general John D. Imboden, at the retreat of the wounded from Gettysburg, Pennsylvania, July 1863*

In 1863 at the Battle of Gettysburg in Pennsylvania, the Union begins to use ambulances. The ambulances are nothing more than wagons pulled by horses. No straw or other padding cushions the wounded men as they are carted over rough fields and roads. But at least they get off the battlefield by the end of the day.

The bullets here are brutal. Rather than going cleanly through the body, they mangle muscles and break bones. They can smash a man's brains or sever his limbs. Often limbs that aren't shot off have to be cut off. Otherwise gangrene, a spreading infection, can kill the wounded man.

Amputations are done by army surgeons at field "hospitals." Any barn, house, or mill that happens to be near (but not too near) a battle can be converted into a hospital. An operating table may be nothing more than a door laid across two barrels. A bucket on the floor catches most of the blood. The surgical instruments look more like shop tools (saws, clamps, and so forth) than medical equipment.

A surgeon performs an amputation in front of a hospital tent in an army camp.

Army surgeons work quickly. An amputation may take minutes, sometimes even seconds, to complete. You will be grateful for their speed, since patients receive little or no anesthesia to deaden their pain.

In this era, people don't understand the importance of sterile (germ-free) instruments in preventing infection. So surgeons use scalpels and saws, wipe them off, and quickly use them again on another patient. One wounded Union soldier wrote that he insisted on staying in the field instead of going to a hospital. He thought he was better off dying by "rebel bullets" than by "Union quackery."

Confederate soldiers suffer even more. The Union blockade prevents many medicines and other medical supplies from getting through to the South. The South also lacks ambulances and trained surgeons. Doctors have to do their best. Many resort to old herbal remedies. They use the herb jimsonweed as a painkiller and sassafras as a stimulant.

LOCAL DISEASES & DANGERS

If you travel as a soldier, you'll have to watch out for dangerous diseases. Disease spreads quickly in the crowded army camps. The sanitation is poor and the diet is unhealthy. Soldiers often camp in places where mosquitoes, flies, and rats thrive and spread disease.

Cholera is the most feared disease. The first symptoms are diarrhea, vomiting, and cramps. The victim's hands and feet may turn cold and dark. Cholera progresses quickly. Its victims can seem fine in the morning and be dead by evening. Cholera spreads when people touch or eat things contaminated by sewage. To avoid getting cholera, wash your hands often. Eat only cooked vegetables. And avoid drinking the water.

You may hear about "camp fever." Camp fever is actually typhoid, a disease that kills fifty thousand soldiers during the war. Malaria, pneumonia, dysentery, and smallpox are also deadly threats. Smallpox patients at one Confederate hospital in Virginia are kept separate from other patients. Only one surgeon is willing to visit their house in the woods. He keeps a set of clothes in the woods and changes into them before entering the "pesthouse." He says, "No one can know how horrible it [smallpox] is unless they experience what I did, not the least being the disgusting and unmistakable odor that attends particularly bad cases."

TAKE IT from a Local

I could not help comparing the surgeons to fiends. It was dark & the building lighted partially with candles . . . near and around the tables stood surgeons with blood all over them and by the side of the tables was a heap of feet, legs and arms.

—*a wounded colonel*

I never came in contact with such gigantic cannibals, such mammoth blood suckers, such unprincipled gluttons.
—*Lieutenant John V. Hadley of Indiana, commenting on the mosquitoes along the Rappahannock River in Virginia*

Even relatively mild diseases can be a danger. Most soldiers, both North and South, are country folk. They have never been exposed to diseases, such as measles, that are common in cities. They lack resistance to these diseases and can develop dangerous complications.

The "quick-step" (diarrhea) is far more serious than the version you may have had. As many as one million soldiers experience it. It kills as many as typhoid.

DISASTERS, CATASTROPHES, & OTHER ANNOYANCES

In the heat of battle, soldiers sometimes accidentally shoot someone on their own side. The most famous mistake of this kind happened to General Stonewall Jackson. He was accidentally shot by his own men and eventually died from his wounds.

You also need to be careful of accidents in camp. Men make mistakes while loading and unloading guns or handling ammunition. Guns go off and torpedoes explode unexpectedly, killing many soldiers. One group of Union soldiers unloaded what they thought were barrels of pork from a railroad car. The barrels actually contained torpedoes. Two barrels collided, causing an explosion that was heard twenty miles away. What little remained of the men was scraped together and placed in hardtack boxes for burial.

You will find it is nearly impossible to avoid becoming infested with lice (small blood-sucking insects that live on humans and other animals). Soldiers refer to lice as "graybacks." In addition, you'll probably encounter chiggers, wood ticks, sand fleas, and other aggravating insects.

If you go in for unusual forms of entertainment, you may enjoy one aspect of insect infestation. Confederate troops race lice, betting on the outcome of the competitions. Some troops stage battles between competing teams of head lice. This spectator sport requires sharp eyesight and a strong stomach.

WATCH FOR RIOTS

Avoid visiting New York City in July 1863. Many people there are angry over unfair draft procedures. Wealthy men can avoid being drafted by paying a fee or hiring a substitute. Poor men have no choice but to go to war. People who live in the poorest parts of New York believe they are forced to give "poor man's blood for a rich man's war."

Local people who sympathize with the South encourage this outrage. They tell draftees that the war will free slaves who will then take their jobs.

The worst resentment spills out when a mob of about five hundred people storms the draft office. They destroy all the draft records. Then they charge into neighboring streets. More people join the fray, and police can't manage the mobs. Rioters burn down an orphanage for black children. At least thirty African Americans are shot, hanged, or stomped to death. In the end, nearly two thousand people get hurt. Finally troops returning from Gettysburg bring the riot under control.

Skyrocketing prices in Charleston, South Carolina, cause another riot in April 1863. People there are disgusted over soaring food bills. They storm into stores and help themselves. This riot is called the "bread riot." Looters seize not only bread but also jewelry, clothing, and other items.

LAW & ORDER

Street crime can be a problem in the cities. If you spend time in New York, for example, you'll find that many citizens carry guns to protect themselves. Robberies are common (even more so after the war). Avoid walking alone at night. Be wary of strangers (as a stranger yourself, you will find people are suspicious of you).

You should be particularly careful about your behavior if you are traveling as a soldier. The most serious crimes are murder, rape, treason, and striking a superior. Desertion (running away from the army) is also taken seriously. Soldiers who commit any of these crimes may be shot by a firing squad. Sometimes soldiers guilty of a serious offense are hung by the thumbs or branded (burned with a hot iron).

Less serious misdeeds such as stealing are punished with imprisonment, hard labor, reduced pay, and smaller food rations. Another popular punishment is "riding the horse." The offender is forced to spend hours painfully straddled across a log high in the air. The log may be decorated to resemble a horse. This punishment is as humiliating as it is uncomfortable.

Other embarrassments include being forced to wear a barrel (a "wooden overcoat") or a sign labeling the wearer as a "coward" or "thief." Some offenders have to drag around a heavy cannonball attached to their leg by a chain. Still others must carry a heavy log or bag of bricks.

Minor offenses against officers are punished severely. Don't talk back or refuse to obey an officer's orders. One of the worst punishments is to

Two soldiers "ride the horse" in Vicksburg, Mississippi.

be bucked and gagged. The offender is made to sit with his hands tied together and slipped over his knees. Then a stick is placed under his knees and above his arms, locking him in position. A stick is then tied in his mouth to gag him. Prisoners are sometimes left like this for hours.

If you think getting punished by your own side is bad, you don't want to be caught by the enemy. Prisoners of war are guilty of fighting for the other side. If you become a prisoner of war, you'll be sent to a prison. Both the Union and the Confederacy have trouble feeding their own soldiers. Prisoners of war are often the last men to get food rations. Your chance of dying in a prison is even greater than dying in battle.

At one prison for Confederate soldiers, nearly one-fourth of the prisoners die. (Some reports put the figure higher—close to one-third.) Conditions are even worse at a Union prison in Rock Island, Illinois. The death rate there is more than 77 percent.

The most famous Civil War prison is in Andersonville, Georgia. More than thirteen thousand Union men die as prisoners there. And it's no wonder. For most prisoners, the only protection from bitter cold or blistering sun comes from a few tree branches, some scraps of wood, or a piece of blanket. Water comes from a contaminated stream. The food is mainly cornmeal with the cobs ground in. Union general William T. Sherman finally captures Atlanta in 1864 and frees the prisoners in nearby Andersonville. They look more like skeletons than human beings.

WHO'S WHO IN CIVIL WAR AMERICA

CLARA BARTON

Clara Barton is one of many women who volunteer as nurses during the war. Some people question whether it is proper for women to work in a grim place like an army hospital. But Clara Barton says nursing the wounded is no more "rough and unseemly for a woman" than fighting is for a man.

Barton dives into the hard work of fighting a war. She is a terrific shot with a revolver, and she can drive a wagon train. She is the first nurse to go to wounded men at the front. For her courage, she is nicknamed the "Angel of the Battlefield." Strong, capable, and independent, she prefers to work alone to get a job done.

Clara Barton doesn't limit herself to nursing. She finds out that a former prisoner of Andersonville prison kept records of the men who died there. So she goes to Andersonville, taking the former prisoner, a crew of gravediggers, and forty coffin makers with her. Then she organizes the job of digging up, identifying, and properly burying thousands of bodies. After the war, she will travel to Europe to study a new organization, the International Red Cross. She will found the American Red Cross in 1882.

ULYSSES S. GRANT

If you visit in 1861, you will find few people have heard of Ulysses S. Grant. This changes in February 1862, after Grant's bold attack on the Confederates at Fort Henry and Fort Donelson in Tennessee. Grant wins an unconditional surrender and captures eleven thousand five hundred Confederate soldiers.

In 1864 President Abraham Lincoln asks Grant to command all the Union armies, and Grant launches an all-out campaign to destroy the

Confederacy. Because so many Union soldiers get killed, some people criticize Grant's aggressive, risky strategies. But he presses on. On April 9, 1865, Grant accepts Robert E. Lee's surrender, ending the Civil War.

After the war, Grant is named General of the Army—a title previously awarded only to George Washington—and serves two terms as president of the United States from 1869 to 1877. He dies on July 23, 1885.

ROBERT E. LEE

You will probably find Robert E. Lee atop his large gray horse, Traveller. (Early in the war, you may hear Traveller called "Jeff Davis" or "Greenbrier.") Robert E. Lee becomes commander of the Confederate Army of Northern Virginia in 1862. But he is a strange choice for the position. He never wanted the South to secede from the Union. And he opposes slavery. He is fighting for the Confederates because he feels loyal to Virginia, his home state.

Lee is a brilliant strategist. Even with fewer soldiers, he leads effective attacks on Union forces. His men love and admire him. So do others who support the Confederate cause. After the war, Lee is charged with treason (betraying his nation). He is never brought to trial, however. He serves as president of Washington College in Lexington, Virginia, until his death in 1870. His last words are "Strike the tent."

ABRAHAM LINCOLN

Abraham Lincoln considers himself a servant of the American people. So he makes himself easily available. He is always interested in ordinary people's opinions of the war.

Locals are impressed that Lincoln visits army camps frequently. He is just as likely to drop in after a defeat as before or after a victory. He often talks to common soldiers. To show his respect for them, he removes his hat. Notice that he merely touches his hat when officers salute him. Lincoln also visits field hospitals. He often insists on talking to nearly every soldier. He shakes hands with many men.

Lincoln often dresses in black. He may wear the familiar stovepipe hat. You'll find he looks worn and tired, particularly late in the war. The pictures you've seen do not do him justice.

On September 22, 1862, Lincoln issues the Emancipation Proclamation. This document states that slaves in Confederate territory are free as of January 1, 1863. It does not free slaves in Union territory. The Confederates ignore the proclamation, so it actually frees no one. But it does keep England and France from lending help to the Confederacy (they don't want to look as if they support slavery). The end of slavery doesn't come until after the war, when the Thirteenth Amendment to the U.S. Constitution is passed in 1865.

HARRIET TUBMAN

You may know of Harriet Tubman as a conductor on the Underground Railroad. The Underground Railroad is not underground, of course. It's a series of houses and other stopping places from the South to the Northern states and Canada where escaping slaves can find shelter. As a conductor, Harriet Tubman leads more than three hundred slaves to freedom. She also works in refugee camps for escaping slaves. For a while, she works as a nurse, caring for both whites and blacks, soldiers and slaves.

Harriet Tubman is short, missing several front teeth, and wears a bandanna on her head. Many slave women have the same description, so she is difficult to recognize. She uses this fact to sneak through Confederate territory. She gathers valuable information for the Union, reporting the locations of ammunition depots, cotton warehouses, and slaves awaiting freedom.

Despite her hard and dangerous work, Harriet Tubman is paid only two hundred dollars over three years. She supports herself by selling pies, gingerbread, and root beer. One Union general later tells Congress that she deserves a pension (pay for wartime service). She gets it—but not until 1892.

PREPARING FOR THE TRIP

EXPERIENCE CARTOMANIA

During the Civil War, many people carried and collected *cartes de visite*. Visitors took these small cards with them when calling at an office or at a friend's house. If no one was in, callers left cards to show they had dropped by. A photograph of the caller was usually on the front of the card, and the caller often signed the back of the card before leaving it.

Some photographers began making portraits of famous people, printing them on cards, and selling them. Collectors could buy the cards and display them in photograph albums. The hobby of collecting *cartes de visite* became so popular that people began calling it "cartomania." To experience cartomania, you will need:

pictures   colored pencils or markers
3 x 5 plain white index cards

Begin by cutting pictures of your favorite celebrities out of magazines or newspapers. Better yet, try to find portraits of people or scenes from the Civil War. If you can print images from the Internet, check out the Civil

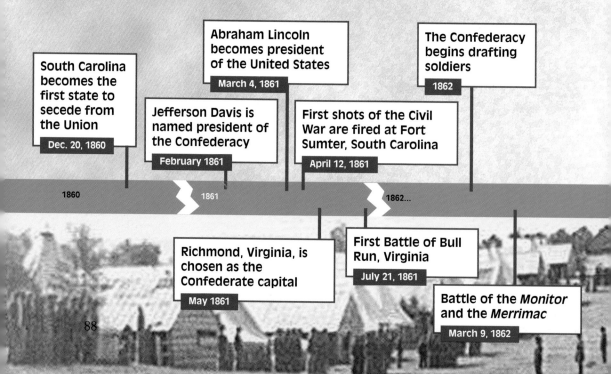

South Carolina becomes the first state to secede from the Union
Dec. 20, 1860

Abraham Lincoln becomes president of the United States
March 4, 1861

The Confederacy begins drafting soldiers
1862

Jefferson Davis is named president of the Confederacy
February 1861

First shots of the Civil War are fired at Fort Sumter, South Carolina
April 12, 1861

1860   1861   1862...

Richmond, Virginia, is chosen as the Confederate capital
May 1861

First Battle of Bull Run, Virginia
July 21, 1861

Battle of the *Monitor* and the *Merrimac*
March 9, 1862

War pictures at <http://lcweb2.loc.gov/ammem/cwphome.html>. You can also use your own school portraits.

Glue the portraits or pictures onto the index cards. Draw a fancy scroll or other border around the edge of each card. On the back, write the name of the person or scene shown. If you're using your own portrait, autograph the back. Then exchange your cards. If a group of friends or a whole class makes the cards, you can do a lot of trading!

HELP YOURSELF TO HARDTACK

Civil War soldiers ate hardtack almost every day. Commercial bakeries prepared it in huge quantities and shipped it to the troops. This scaled-down recipe is used by modern groups who get together to re-create Civil War scenes. You will need:

> two cups water   flour
> 1 teaspoon salt

Preheat the oven to 400°F. In a large bowl, mix together the water and the salt. Then slowly add flour until the dough doesn't feel sticky. Sprinkle a little more flour on a cutting board and roll out the dough to about half an inch thick. Cut the slab of dough into squares about three inches by three inches. Poke some tiny holes in each square. (The tines of a fork work well to make the holes.) Place the squares of dough on a greased cookie sheet. Then bake for one hour. Yum!

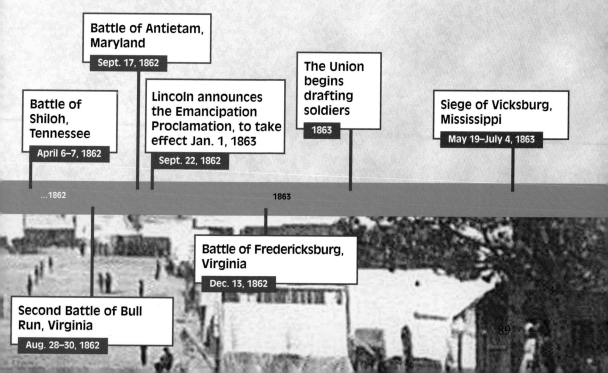

Battle of Antietam, Maryland
Sept. 17, 1862

The Union begins drafting soldiers
1863

Battle of Shiloh, Tennessee
April 6–7, 1862

Lincoln announces the Emancipation Proclamation, to take effect Jan. 1, 1863
Sept. 22, 1862

Siege of Vicksburg, Mississippi
May 19–July 4, 1863

...1862

1863

Battle of Fredericksburg, Virginia
Dec. 13, 1862

Second Battle of Bull Run, Virginia
Aug. 28–30, 1862

89

GLOSSARY

anesthetic: a substance or drug that numbs the body and is usually used to lessen pain during an operation

bayonet: a long steel blade that fits on the end of a rifle and is used by soldiers in close, hand-to-hand combat

bugle: a brass instrument, similar to a trumpet, that is often used for military calls and songs

capitol: a building that is used by a government for meetings and other functions. When this word is capitalized, it refers specifically to the Capitol building in Washington, D.C.

immigrant: a person who has come from his or her native country to live in a different country

kerosene: type of oil usually used to fuel oil lamps

parlor: a room in the front of the house that is used primarily for entertaining guests

plantation: a Southern estate that includes farmland and a house or mansion

regiment: a military unit of troops. In the American Civil War, most regiments had one thousand soldiers, usually all from the same state.

rural: related to country life or farming, as opposed to city life

steamboat: a steam-powered boat that was invented in America in the 1700s and that carried passengers and goods on rivers such as the Mississippi

taps: a military bugle call blown at night when the lights are put out. Taps can also mean a similar bugle call that is played at military funerals.

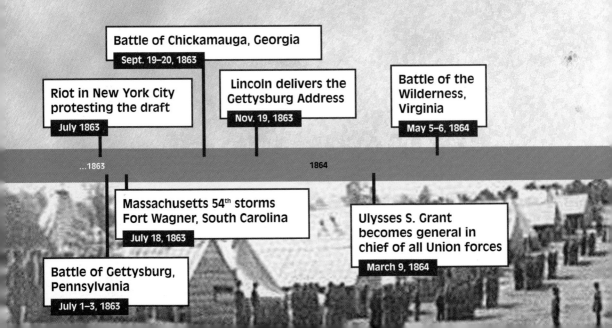

Battle of Chickamauga, Georgia
Sept. 19–20, 1863

Riot in New York City protesting the draft
July 1863

Lincoln delivers the Gettysburg Address
Nov. 19, 1863

Battle of the Wilderness, Virginia
May 5–6, 1864

...1863

1864

Massachusetts 54th storms Fort Wagner, South Carolina
July 18, 1863

Ulysses S. Grant becomes general in chief of all Union forces
March 9, 1864

Battle of Gettysburg, Pennsylvania
July 1–3, 1863

PRONUNCIATION GUIDE

barouche	buh-ROOSH
cholera	KAHL-ur-uh
crinoline	KRIHN-uh-luhn
croquet	kroh-KAY
Potomac	puh-TOH-muhk
privy	PRIH-vee
secede	sih-SEED
sutler	SUHT-lur

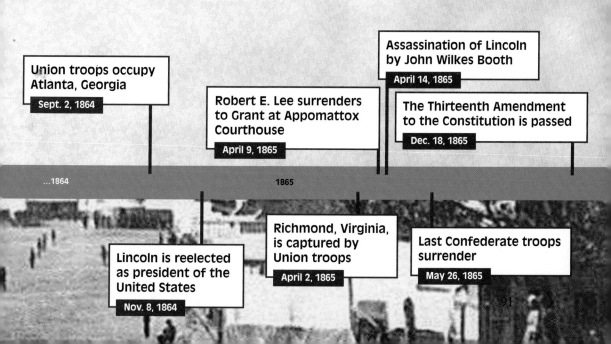

Union troops occupy Atlanta, Georgia
Sept. 2, 1864

Robert E. Lee surrenders to Grant at Appomattox Courthouse
April 9, 1865

Assassination of Lincoln by John Wilkes Booth
April 14, 1865

The Thirteenth Amendment to the Constitution is passed
Dec. 18, 1865

...1864

1865

Lincoln is reelected as president of the United States
Nov. 8, 1864

Richmond, Virginia, is captured by Union troops
April 2, 1865

Last Confederate troops surrender
May 26, 1865

FURTHER READING

Books

Chang, Ina. *A Separate Battle: Women and the Civil War.* New York: Lodestar Books, 1991.

Duane, Damon. *When This Cruel War Is Over: The Civil War Home Front.* Minneapolis: Lerner Publications Company, 1996.

Egger-Bovet, Howard, and Marlene Smith-Baranzini. *Brown Paper School, USKids History: Book of the American Civil War.* Boston: Little Brown & Company, 1998.

Ferris, Jeri. *Go Free or Die: A Story about Harriet Tubman.* Minneapolis: Carolrhoda Books, Inc., 1988.

Ferris, Jeri. *Walking the Road to Freedom: A Story about Sojourner Truth.* Minneapolis: Carolrhoda Books, Inc., 1988.

Greene, Meg. *Slave Young, Slave Long: The American Slave Experience.* Minneapolis: Carolrhoda Books, Inc., 1999.

Haskins, Jim. *Black, Blue & Gray: African Americans in the Civil War.* New York: Simon & Schuster Books for Young Readers, 1998.

Josephson, Judith Pinkerton. *Allan Pinkerton: The Original Private Eye.* Minneapolis: Lerner Publications Company, 1996.

McPherson, Stephanie Sammartino. *Sisters against Slavery: A Story about Sarah and Angelina Grimké.* Minneapolis: Carolrhoda Books, Inc., 1999.

Moore, Kay. *If You Lived at the Time of the Civil War.* New York: Scholastic, Inc., 1994.

Morris, Jeffrey. *The Lincoln Way.* Minneapolis: Lerner Publications Company, 1996.

Murphy, Jim. *The Boy's War: Confederate and Union Soldiers Talk about the Civil War.* New York: Clarion, 1990.

Internet Sites

"African American Odessy: The Civil War," *American Memory*
<http://memory.loc.gov/ammem/aahotml/exhibit/aopart4.html>

Civil War
<http://www.civilwar.com>

The Civil War Home Page
<http://www.civil-war.net>

Civil War Interactive
<http://www.almshouse.com>

Civil War Traveler
<http://civilwar-va.com>

"The Gettysburg Address," *Library of Congress Exhibits*
<http://lcweb.loc.gov/exhibits/gadd/ga.html>

"Jump Back in Time: Civil War (1860–1865)," *America's Story from America's Library*
<http://americaslibrary.gov/cgi-bin/page.cgi/jb/1860-1865>

The Underground Railroad
<http://www.nationalgeographic.com/features/99/railroad>

BIBLIOGRAPHY

Brooks, Noah. *Washington, D.C., in Lincoln's Time.* Chicago: Quadrangle Books, 1971.

Caton, Bruce. *The American Heritage Picture History of the Civil War.* Edited by Richard M. Ketchum. New York: American Heritage/Bonanza Books, 1982.

Davis, Burke. *The Civil War: Strange & Fascinating Facts.* New York: The Fairfax Press, 1982.

Denney, Robert E. *Civil War Medicine: Care & Comfort of the Wounded.* New York: Sterling Publishing Co., 1995.

Dorf, Philip. *Highlights & Sidelights of the Civil War.* Middletown, CT: Southfarm Press, 1989.

Faust, Drew Gilpin. *Mothers of Invention: Women of the Slaveholding South in the American Civil War.* Chapel Hill, NC: The University of North Carolina Press, 1996.

Foner, Eric, and John A. Garraty, eds. *The Reader's Companion to American History.* Boston: Houghton Mifflin Company, 1991.

Hague, Parthenia Antoinette. *A Blockaded Family: Life in Southern Alabama During the Civil War.* Lincoln, NE: University of Nebraska Press, 1991.

Haskins, Jim. *Black, Blue & Gray: African Americans in the Civil War.* New York: Simon & Schuster Books for Young Readers, 1998.

Kirchberger, Joe H. *The Civil War and Reconstruction: An Eyewitness History.* New York: Facts On File, 1991.

Laugel, Auguste. *The United States During the Civil War.* Bloomington, IN: Indiana University Press, 1961.

Lowenfels, Walter. *Poet Walt Whitman's Civil War.* New York: Alfred A. Knopf, 1960.

McClurg, Alexander C. Unpublished memoir, *Reminiscences of Chicago During the Civil War.* Introduction by Mabel McIlvaine. New York: The Citadel Press, 1967.

McCutcheon, Marc. *The Writer's Guide to Everyday Life in the 1800s.* Cincinnati, OH: Writer's Digest Books, 1993.

Reader's Digest. *Everyday Life Through the Ages.* Pleasantville, NY: Reader's Digest, 1992.

Scott, John Anthony. *The Story of America.* Washington, D.C.: The National Geographic Society, 1984.

Stern, Philip van Doren, ed. *Soldier Life in the Union and Confederate Armies.* Bloomington, IN: Indiana University Press, 1961.

Sutherland, Daniel E. *The Expansion of Everyday Life 1860–1876.* New York: Harper & Row, 1989.

Time-Life Books. *Voices of the Civil War: Soldier Life.* Richmond, VA: Time-Life Books, 1996.

Wiley, Bell I. *The Common Soldier of the Civil War.* New York: Charles Scribner's Sons, 1975.

Wright, Mike. *What They Didn't Teach You about the Civil War.* Novato, CA: Presidio Press, 1996.

INDEX

Photo Acknowledgments
The images in this book are used with the permission of: Library of Congress, pp. 2, 18 [LC-B811-4016], 19[LC-B817-7890], 20 [LC-USA7-5063], 23 [LC-B811-3242], 26 (left) [LC USZ62-40571], 37 [LC-B8184-10186], 38 [LC-B8171-2405], 46–47 [LC-USZ62-3331], 55 [LC-USZ62-7824], 58 [LC-B8171-7745], 61 [LC-B8171-356], 64 [LC-USZ62-79617], 77 [LC-B8171-7636], 86 (top) [LC-BH821-6704], 86 (bottom) [LC-24632-3479], 88–89 [LC-B8171-7733], 90–91 [LC-B8171-7733]; National Archives, pp. 6–7 [NWDNS-165-SC-39], 15 [NWDNS-83-FB-272], 41 [War & Conflict 221], 42–43 [NWDNS-111-B-4817], 48 [NWDNS-111-B-1715], 70 (bottom) [NWDNS-111-B-216], 74 [W&C 231], 79 [W&C 220]; © Collection of The New York Historical Society, p. 10 [47843]; Corbis/Bettmann, pp. 12, 26–27, 68; courtesy of the Hargrett Rare Book and Manuscript Library, University of Georgia Libraries, p. 16; courtesy of the Trustees of the Boston Public Library Rare Books Department, p. 17; copyrighted stamp design reproduced with permission of the U.S. Postal Service, p. 25; IPS/Dan Mahoney, pp. 27 (both), 36 (center); Chicago Historical Society, pp. 28 [ICHi-09304], 31 [ICHi-22,103], 32 [ICHi-29012], 33 [ICHi-31276], 51 [ICHi-22210]; Brown Brothers, pp. 29, 87; Archive Photos, pp. 34, 39; Minnesota Historical Society, pp. 35, 36 (left and right), 71; Virginia Military Institute Archives, p. 44; © Tria Giovan/Corbis, pp. 46 (top), 50, 60, 70 (top), 73 (both); Massachusetts Commandery Military Order of the Loyal Legion and the US Army Military History Institute, p. 49; Scala/Art Resource, pp. 52–53; Culver Pictures, p. 57; National Museum of American Art, Washington, D.C./Art Resource, NY, p. 63; The Society for the Preservation of New England Antiquities, p. 67; Corbis, p. 83.

Front cover: © CORBIS, (top); Minnesota Historical Society (bottom, both).

ABOUT THE AUTHOR

Nancy Day is the author of nine books and forty-five articles for young people. She loves to read and is fascinated with the idea of time travel, which she says is "actually history in a great disguise." Her interest in time travel inspired the Passport to History series. Nancy Day lives with her husband, son, and two cats in a house that was built in 1827—before the Civil War. She often imagines what it would be like to go back in time to meet the shipbuilder who once lived there.

Acknowledgments for Quoted Material pp. 13, 32, as quoted by Drew Gilpin Faust, *Mothers of Invention: Women of the Slaveholding South in the American Civil War* (Chapel Hill, NC: The University of North Carolina Press, 1996); pp. 14, 43, as quoted by Walter Lowenfels, *Poet Walt Whitman's Civil War* (New York: Alfred A. Knopf, 1960); p. 35, as quoted by Mike Wright, *What They Didn't Teach You About the Civil War* (Novato, CA: Presidio Press); p. 38, as quoted by Bell I. Wiley, *The Common Soldier of the Civil War* (New York: Charles Scribner's Sons, 1975); p. 40, as quoted by Daniel E. Sutherland, *The Expansion of Everyday Life 1860–1876* (New York: Harper & Row, 1989); p. 54, as quoted by Eric Foner and John A. Garraty, editors, *The Reader's Companion to American History* (Boston: Houghton Mifflin Company, 1991); p. 64, as quoted by Philip Van Doren Stern, editor, *Soldier Life in the Union and Confederate Armies* (Bloomington, IN: Indiana University Press, 1961); p. 71, as quoted by Time-Life Books, *Voices of the Civil War: Soldier Life* (Richmond, VA: Time-Life Books, 1996); p. 78, as quoted by Robert E. Denney, *Civil War Medicine: Care & Comfort of the Wounded* (New York: Sterling Publishing Co., 1995); p. 80, as quoted by John Anthony Scott, *The Story of America* (Washington, D.C.: The National Geographic Society, 1984).